Aussi tourmenté qu'aimé, Oscar Wilde (1854-1900) a traversé de nombreux aléas pour devenir un dramaturge, auteur et poète de renom. Il est l'un des écrivains les plus influents de l'ère victorienne. Le travail de Wilde est marqué par sa profonde compréhension des aspects positifs de la société comme de ses dangers. Critiqué en raison de sa prétendue « nature efféminée » et opprimé par un monde largement homophobe, Wilde n'a jamais perdu sa résilience. Il a tiré profit de ses expériences pour créer des œuvres littéraires brillantes, quoique controversées.

La comédie *L'Importance d'être Constant*, dont une ébauche est reproduite ici, a rencontré un vif succès jusqu'à ce que Wilde soit emprisonné pour « attentat à la pudeur ». Il s'agit de l'un des premiers procès notoires de célébrités, mais ce n'était, malheureusement, qu'une des nombreuses persécutions d'un membre de la communauté LGBTQ pour un acte consensuel. Nous avions publié ce Manuscrit Estampé en 2010 et nous le réintégrons à la collection pour célébrer l'héritage littéraire de Wilde et sa persévérance.

Oscar Wilde, missliebig und gefeiert zugleich, durchlief ein Leben voller Höhen und Tiefen, um zu einem Schriftsteller von Weltrang zu werden, der als einer der einflussreichsten Autoren der viktorianischen Zeit gilt.

Wildes Werk ist mit Einsichten eines Mannes gespickt, der die Vorzüge und Gefahren der Gesellschaft genau kannte. Kritik an seinem als „weiblich" betrachteten Wesen und der Unterdrückung durch eine zu großen Teilen homophobe Welt hielt er stand. Aus seinen Erfahrungen brachte er brillante, wenn auch umstrittene, literarische Werke hervor.

Die Komödie *The Importance of Being Earnest*, von der wir hier einen Entwurf sehen, war zunächst ein großer Erfolg, wurde nach Wildes Verurteilung zum Zuchthaus wegen „Unzucht" aber gekürzt. Es handelte sich zwar um eines der ersten Verfahren einer berühmten Persönlichkeit, leider aber nur um einen vieler Fälle von Verfolgung einer Person aus der LGBTQ-Community. Wildes literarischen Erbes und Ausdauer zu Ehren präsentieren wir diese Faszinierende Handschrift, die wir erstmals 2010 veröffentlichten, nun erneut.

Oscar Wilde (1854-1900) visse un'esistenza complessa che lo convertì in drammaturgo, scrittore e poeta di fama mondiale e In uno degli scrittori più influenti dell'epoca vittoriana.

L'opera di Wilde, autore con una profonda comprensione sia degli aspetti positivi che dei pericoli della società, è ricca di intuizioni. Criticato per quella che era percepita come "natura effeminata" e oppresso da un mondo estremamente omofobo, Wilde non si arrese, e utilizzò le sue esperienze per scrivere opere letterarie brillanti e controverse.

La commedia *L'importanza di chiamarsi Ernesto*, la cui bozza è qui riprodotta, venne accolta molto positivamente al momento dell'esordio, tuttavia il successo dell'opera subì un brusco arresto quando Wilde fu condannato per "grave indecenza". Il processo, uno dei primi che coinvolgeva un personaggio famoso, fu solo una delle tante persecuzioni di un membro della comunità LGBTQ+. Proponiamo di nuovo questo design della serie Preziosi Manoscritti, già pubblicato nel 2010, per celebrare l'eredità letteraria e la perseveranza di Oscar Wilde.

Oscar Wilde (1854-1900), atormentado y admirado a partes iguales, tuvo una vida de altibajos hasta alcanzar la fama como dramaturgo, escritor y poeta. Es sin duda uno de los autores más influyentes de la literatura victoriana.

La obra de Wilde está marcada por sus profundas reflexiones tanto de los aspectos positivos como de los peligros de la sociedad. Criticado por lo que se percibía como «carácter afeminado» y oprimido por un mundo homófobo, Wilde demostró una gran resiliencia y aprovechó sus experiencias para crear obras literarias tan brillantes como polémicas.

Aquí reproducimos un borrador de la comedia *La importancia de llamarse Ernesto*, que tuvo un éxito arrollador desde su estreno, poco antes de que Wilde fuera condenado a prisión por «indecencia grave». Fue uno de los primeros juicios mediáticos de la historia, y lamentablemente no el único en el que una persona de la comunidad LGBTQ era perseguida por su orientación sexual. En 2010 lanzamos este diseño de la colección Manuscritos Bellos, y esta temporada lo recuperamos para celebrar el legado literario de Wilde y su perseverancia personal.

paperblanks®
EMBELLISHED
MANUSCRIPTS

Wilde, The Importance of Being Earnest

A man as tormented as he was beloved, Oscar Wilde (1854–1900) overcame a life of extraordinary ups and downs to become a world-renowned playwright, author and poet. He stands as one of the most influential writers of the Victorian era.

Wilde's work is fraught with the insights of a man who possessed a deep understanding of both the positives and perils of society. Criticized for what was perceived as an "effeminate nature" and oppressed by a largely homophobic world, Wilde remained resilient. He used his experiences to form brilliant, if controversial, literary works.

The comedy *The Importance of Being Earnest*, a draft of which is reproduced here, was a great success upon opening but saw its run cut short when Wilde was imprisoned for "gross indecency." This represented one of the first famous celebrity trials but was, sadly, only one of many persecutions of a member of the LGBTQ community for a consensual act. We first released this Embellished Manuscript in 2010, and this season we bring it back in celebration of Wilde's literary legacy and personal perseverance.

ISBN: 978-1-4397-9364-0
ULTRA FORMAT   144 PAGES   LINED
DESIGNED IN CANADA